THINGS I WANT TO SAY AT WORK BUT CAN'T

A FUNNY SWEAR WORD ADULT COLORING BOOK

COLOR TEST PAGE

COLOR TEST PAGE

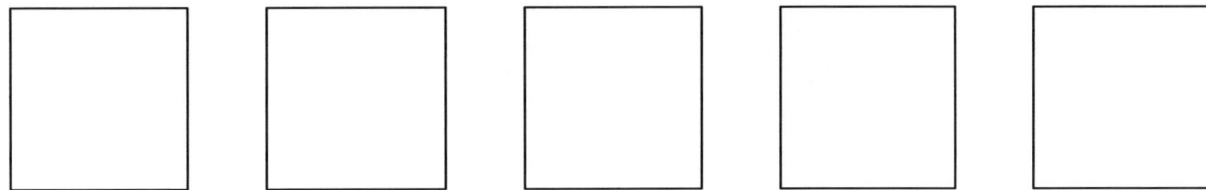

I GIVE JUST ENOUGH FUCKS TO STAY EMPLOYED

dealing with your bullshit isn't in my job description

it would be a good shift today ...oh, look, a clusterfuck

I'm not feeling feeling worky today

CAUTION:

TO AVOID INJURY, DON'T TELL ME HOW TO DO MY JOB

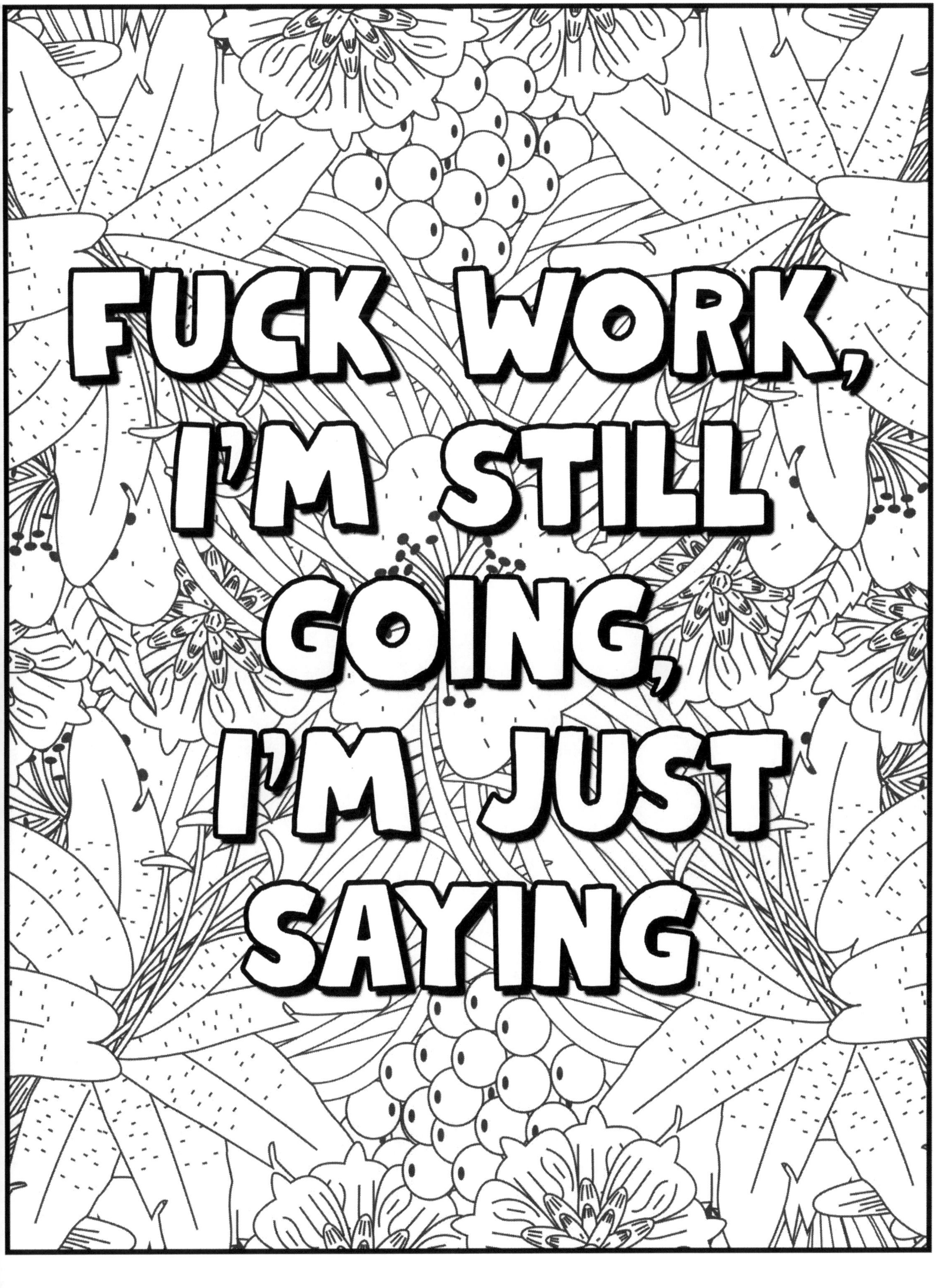
FUCK WORK,
I'M STILL
GOING,
I'M JUST
SAYING

I'm Only Being Nice To You Because I'm At Work

TOP OF THE MORNING TO YOU FUCKERS

It's a beautiful day to leave me alone

NOT MY CIRCUS NOT MY MONKEYS

SORRY I'M LATE.... I DIDN'T WANT TO COME

LET'S KEEP THE DUMBFUCKERY TO A MINIMUM TODAY

sometimes i can't tell if i'm in preschool or highschool. oh wait, I'm at work

WHO HIRED THIS BITCH?

FUCK YOU VERY MUCH !!

DON'T APPROACH MY DESK UNLESS YOU WANT A STAPLER UP YOUR ASS

You are not the supervisor go sit ASS down

i SURViVED ANOTHER MEETING THAT SHOULD HAVE BEEN AN EMAIL

Things i hate about my job:

1) Getting out Of bed,
2) People,
3) Working.

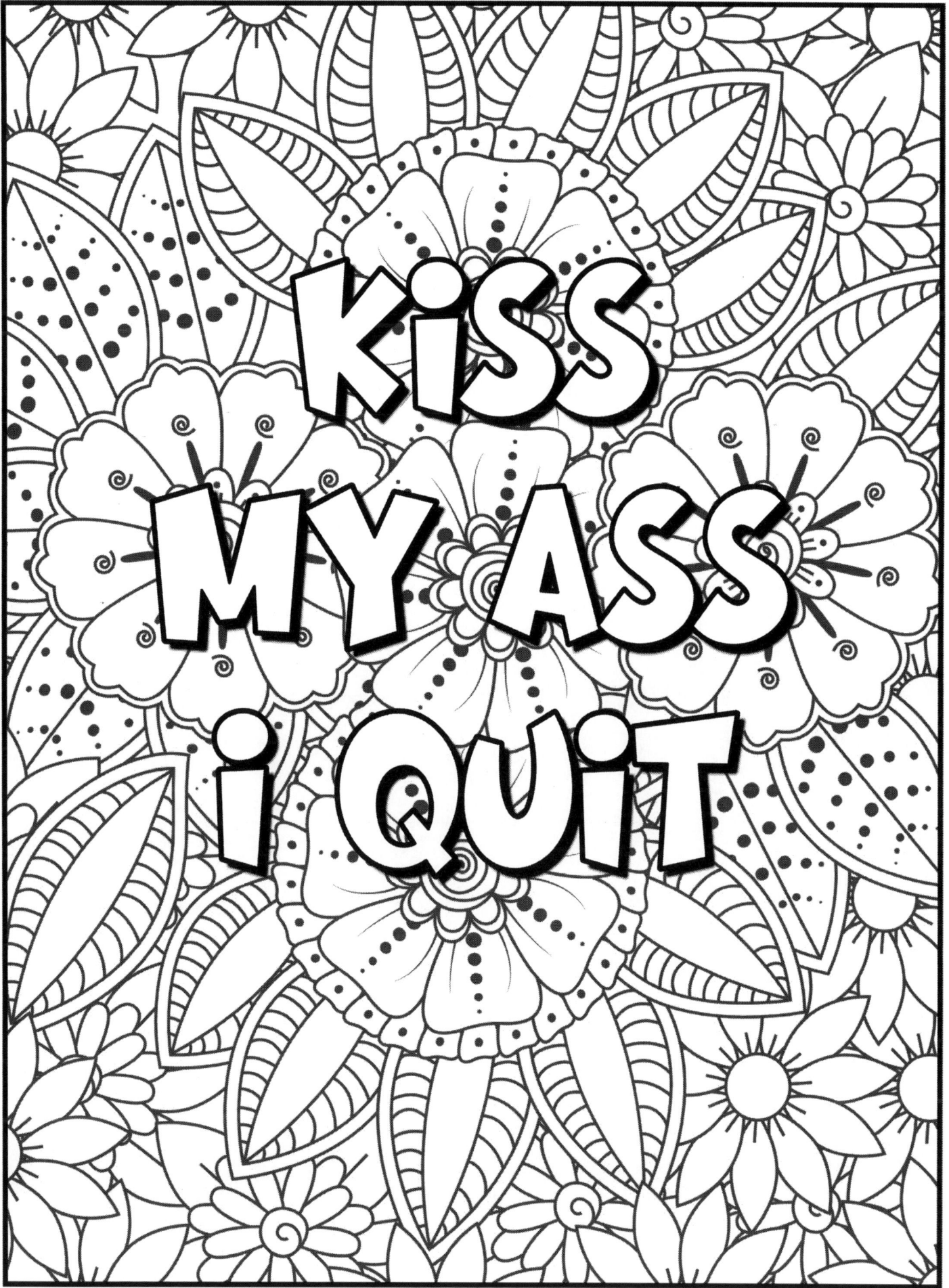

KISS MY ASS I QUIT

Oh look, nobody gives a fuck

I'm Not rude i just say what everyone else think

you should
smile
frequently
the boss
likes idiots

I express
my emotions
by saying
"fuck"
in various
tones

Looks Like it's fuck this shit o'clock

I CAN'T BE HELD RESPONSIBLE FOR WHAT MY FACE DOES WHEN YOU TALK

i DON'T THINK THERE WILL BE ENOUGH COFFEE OR ENOUGH MIDDLE FINGERS FOR THIS MONDAY

HERE'S ANOTHER DAY OF OUTWARD SMILES AND INWARD RAGE SCREAMS

THANKS FOR YOUR COMPLAINT. I WILL FILE IT RIGHT BETWEEN "DON'T GIVE A FLYING FUCK" AND "SUCKS TO BE YOU"

I'm not doing shit today

Printed in Great Britain
by Amazon